REFLECTIONS
ON LIFE

REFLECTIONS ON LIFE

Pocket Philosophy

Patricia B. Schoeler

Library of Congress Control Number: 2023905120

ISBN: 978-1-960093-30-1   (Paperback)
ISBN: 978-1-960093-31-8   (E-Book)

Printed in the United States of America

Contents

CHAPTER 2   FAMILY WOES?

CHAPTER 3   LOSS AND FAITH

CHAPTER 4   LIFE'S LITTLE MOMENTS

CHAPTER 5   LESSONS LEARNED

Also by Patricia B. Schoeler:

The Day America Cried!
So Many Innocents Died
9-11-01

Grief Hurts

To Marie Stopfer, whose encouragement, input, and belief in my work has given me the courage to follow my dreams, wherever they may lead me.

Special thanks to Marie Stopfer, Connie Williams, Jack Healy, and Barbara Hogan Devlin for their sage advice, close scrutiny, and valued opinions during the compilation of this book.

Introduction

Life happens to all of us. Most times it is wonderful. However, there are times we run into the "speed bumps of life." Sometimes these "bumps" can be high indeed, sending us quite a jolt. Others are minor, and we manage to ride over them with relative ease. Thankfully, not all these incidences happen to us directly, but we can be deeply affected when it happens to our loved ones, be it family or friends.

The important thing to remember is, we are not in this alone. We may think we are, but others have traveled this road before us.

It is my hope that these poems will offer comfort and insight into these mysteries of life.

CHAPTER ONE

INSPIRATIONAL

Our Experiences

We are the product of our upbringing and experiences from the past
The impact they had on us, really does last

Thoughts that race through our minds; the memories they bring
All have a big part in our reactions to things

Some give us pleasure; some give us pain
These things will happen to us again and again

We are never given more than we can bear
Problems happen to all of us; accept your share

As life happens around us, we learn how to cope
Keep your sense of humor and always have hope!

Serenity!

There is an expression, take time to smell the roses
But we are always in such a hurry; this a problem poses

This morning I noticed a leaf filled with the morning dew
The sunlight made it glisten; Mother Nature's show just for you

I watched a spider web swaying in the morning breeze
It was sparkling brightly; a sight like this is sure to please

Through the wet grass I followed my little pup
His fun and his innocence lift my spirits up

Early morning walks are so quiet and serene
Time to pause and reflect; even the air smells clean

You really owe it to yourself to make the time
I did this morning and it gave me peace of mind!

Patricia B. Schoeler

Grow Where You Are Planted

Change is the one thing you can count on in life
Sometimes it is happy, sometimes it causes strife

My niece was moving out of state
Due to a job opportunity for her mate

Any life change can be scary yet exciting
Actually a new beginning can be quite inviting

"Grow where you are planted" was advice my sister gave
It's advice that can work from birth to grave

Establishing roots, we do it all the time
Every time circumstances change, yours and mine

Remember leaving Mom for the first day of school?
Trying so hard to be brave 'cause crying isn't cool

Most of us had to change schools once or twice
Again something new, it was kind of nice

We made new friends along the way
Some at school or from church where we'd pray

We went out to work to earn a living
Once again we started a new beginning

Sometimes we are so comfortable the way things are
That we're not willing to venture very far

Whenever there was change we had to adjust
"Grow where we are planted" really was a must

We are learning and growing each and every day
All combined experiences make us who we are today

Like a tree we sometimes twist and turn in the breeze
With roots deep enough we can face it with relative ease

A stranger may be a friend we haven't been introduced to yet
Hey, what can you lose; give it a try and see what you get

Be open to experiences that may be new
It may be the best thing that happened to you!

Patricia B. Schoeler

Day At A Time

A day at a time is all you can do
When life throws too much stress at you

When you break it down into 24 small hours
It gives you the feeling of holding some powers

You can do most anything if the time seems small
You'll discover it's not necessary to complete it all

Break it down to pieces that are realistic
You can get it done that way without going ballistic!

Angels We Meet

There are angel's we meet along the way
To help guide us through our day

They may not be apparent; we may not know who they are
But when we are in need, they are never very far

They offer comfort and guidance, extending a helping hand
To help clear our minds, to help us understand

Not always in spirit but taking a human form
Not always to our expectations do they conform

Ever wonder why *fate* placed us in a particular spot?
Is this by *plan* or *coincidence* or not?

Some people come into your life for only a little while
And when they are gone they are remembered with a gentle smile

Keep your heart and mind open for you may never know
You too may be someone's *angel* offering comfort wherever you go!

Patricia B. Schoeler

The Power Within!

"Hope" is a word meaning "looking forward to"
We all had things we've hoped for, our whole life through

Hope gives us power to face what lies ahead
Hope allows us to look beyond what we face with dread

It is a promise of what is yet to be
A dream that our minds-eye can see

It's important to never underestimate the power of prayer
Or how many people love you, how much they care

Faith and hope go hand and hand
Giving us power to endure what we don't understand

Life can be short; we know it's unpredictable
Some parts wonderful, some parts despicable

When times are rough and you're feeling down
It's comforting to have family and friends around

Don't waste today in despair and sorrow
Live life as if you'll have a wonderful tomorrow!

Our Childhood

As kids we led such protected lives
Given opportunities to be sure we'd thrive

Our parents loved us and kept us safe
And would do most anything to put a smile on our face

Over the years though, our problems grew
A ritual of life; things we all must go through

We have to take the bad along with the good
We learn to compromise and to empathize, as well we should

How can we help others if we've never felt pain?
We get bounced around but we get up again

Look at all our blessings; just too many to count
We wouldn't give them up for any amount

A positive attitude keeps us healthy and strong
Our upbringing and our faith carried us along

So yes, we've been badly hurt, but we survived it all
And our happy times are plentiful if you sit back and recall!

Patricia B. Schoeler

Calm After The Storm

The storm crashed wildly over my head
The violence of it all filled me with dread

My puppy trembled and jumped into my arms
Sure the world was ending; he was filled with alarm

Together we sat and rode out the storm
Waiting for it to stop, knowing this is not the norm

Life does that; tosses us around
But somehow we end up with our feet on the ground

The sun *does* come out and wash away the bad
Embrace all the good out there and don't be sad

If we don't experience the *storms*, how can we appreciate the good?
I'm sure all of us would like to avoid pain if only we could

But that's not how it works; it's not how it goes
Why some get more than others only heaven knows

Live life to the fullest and enjoy each day
There's always something to smile about and take time to pray!

True Love

True love is not abusive in word or in deed
Humor and respect, important to succeed

Kind, considerate, allowing you to grow
Knowing you are loved, no matter where you go

Another major ingredient is a large dose of trust
Without that, many relationships go bust

Thoughtful, intuitive, understanding, giving you space
A warm loving feeling that leaves a smile on your face

It's great to have all this passion mixed in with devotion
Blessed are those who have found this wonderful emotion!

Patricia B. Schoeler

Savor Every Minute

Enjoy life now, savor every single minute
Love and embrace everyone who is in it

We have no idea when we offer a warm smile
We may have brightened someone's day for a little while

The power held in just the touch of a hand
Saying "It's ok, I'm here, I understand"

The sound of your laughter on someone's ear
May be just the thing they needed to hear

Never underestimate the power you possess
Or the opportunity you have to bring happiness

Because before you know it, the present becomes the past
It's a fact of life that not all things are meant to last

Relationships do become deeper, so change isn't necessarily bad
Wonderful things do happen, so don't waste time with being sad

Memories can be wonderful; they make up who we are
And the effect they have can carry us very far

People touch our lives in a very special way
Some good, some bad at work or home or play

Life experiences teach us what we know
It's how we learn; it's how we grow!

Happiness and Peace

Wouldn't it be great, this Christmas cheer
If only we could carry the feeling throughout the year?

We greet each other with a smile on our face
For those we love we include a warm embrace

We do our best to show we care
We seem so much more willing to give and to share

Our spirits are lifted; our spirits are high
It's *that* time of year so we don't question why

But it's our frame of mind that makes us feel good
We look beyond ourselves, helping others as well we should

This is something we should strive for, a goal we should set
For the more happiness you give, the more you are sure to get!

Patricia B. Schoeler

Age Is Only A Number

The older we get; we don't always like what we see
We look in the mirror; "Is that really me?"

When did the wrinkles settle onto my face?
My body has lumps now that seem out of place

Even my hair is turning gray
I sure didn't plan for things to turn out this way

Too many loved ones have now passed away
And are no longer here to enjoy another day

Others are sick, not sure of what their future will hold
Powerless to stop these problems as they unfold

But, then I take stock of all I have done
And I'm still here on earth and having fun

Looking at the alternatives my outlook becomes clear
God has blessed me with another day and I am still here

So, don't look in that mirror, act like you feel inside
Age is only a number, so wear it with pride!

Too Busy!

Finding true friendship is indeed a treasure
It is a relationship full of warmth and pleasure

Of being there for each other through thick and thin
This feeling of companionship comes from deep within

When things are great, you laugh together
Sharing secrets that you will protect forever

But, like anything, it needs to be nurtured and tended
Due to neglect, many relationships have ended

Never be "too busy" to make a quick call
The conversation doesn't have to be long at all

See how they're doing, if everything is OK
Then promise to call when you can talk another day

We all have our days that are crazy and full of strife
But you must decide the importance friends represent in your life

The message you are sending is, "I don't have time for you"
Is that really what you want to do?

Make that connection now, before it's too late
Don't leave it to chance; don't leave it to fate!

Patricia B. Schoeler

Story To Tell!

Everyone you see has a story to tell
Some people are healthy; some are not well

Some may have lives that are truly blessed
Others may suffer more than you could have guessed

Not always is everything the way it may appear
An unfriendly act may be hiding a fear

How about giving a smile when you pass their way
It may be just what they need to make their day

An act of kindness that may help you too
For what you give has a way of coming back to you!

Who Knows What Tomorrow Will Bring?

Not one of us knows what tomorrow will bring
Will it make us sad or make us sing?

If we fret about tomorrow, then we will lose today
Certainly we can't change what happened yesterday

Today is a gift we are meant to enjoy and live
Put everything you have into it, give all you have to give

Learn from whatever has *not* gone your way
Enjoy the good times; learn how to play

Life is not a rehearsal; it's your one and only chance
Take time to look at life, not just give a passing glance

Have no regrets; let your loved ones know you care
It will be too late when they are no longer there

Each day has twenty-four hours, so give it your best
Laugh, love and be happy before you lay down to rest!

Patricia B. Schoeler

Life's Roller Coaster

Sometimes emotions are like a roller coaster ride
First you're riding high; then on a very scary slide

Life is like that, I always say
It's how we learn; it's not always play

Sometimes it's frightening how low we can go
But things get better again, this we know

Just ride it out and wait and see
Soon everything will be the way it should be!

Saying Good-bye To A Friend!

How do you say good-bye to a friend?
It hurts a lot, I won't pretend

Memories of good times flood through my mind
Many experiences are one of a kind

I'm reminded of something said by the priest at mass
Something powerful to think about, and not to let pass

Certain people enter our lives, we're not always aware of who they are
Who are meant to journey with us for only so far

Who can say what the reason might be
It may take a long time for us to see

Some journeys are short; some are long
But the emotions they evoke are really quite strong

An anonymous quote came over the Internet
A profound statement, as deep as you can get

"Don't cry because it's over; smile because it happened"
A deep, yet easy, concept for us to comprehend

Let's enjoy our friends and treasure each moment we share
For the truth is that they may not always be there

Take the time to keep in touch
To both of you it can mean so much!

Patricia B. Schoeler

So Disappointed!

Sometimes people disappoint us, we don't always understand why
We can't figure it out no matter how hard we try

What they want now, may be different than before
Circumstances change, they may not need us anymore

If you keep getting rebuffed and turned away
If they reject your offers to go eat or to play

Try hard to think if you've done something wrong
If you're sure you didn't, then perhaps you should move along

I guess in a way it's their problem to bear
But it still hurts us, because we really do care

They may not realize that what they do
Can have an impact on others too

Mourn the loss of a friendship gone awry
You have done your best but you may never know why!

This Wonderful Ride!

Life can be this most wonderful ride
The start we are given, isn't ours to decide

Some have a head start; others may lag behind
But we all have the power of a legacy, you will find

We all enter this world with a very clean slate
The potential is there, so is the power to be great

We won't all be a Nobel Prize winner or a movie star
But a champion when others respect what we do and who we are

The love and memories left behind will determine our worth
So yes, we do leave our footprints on this earth!

Patricia B. Schoeler

Way Back When!

Remember when your parents gave you that withering look?
You knew you did wrong; in your boots you shook

Maybe they said, "I'm going to count to three"
We completed the task; we didn't wait to see

Or perhaps you got the infamous pinch
Warning you to sit still and not move one inch!

Things have changed so much in this day and age
It's not a clear path working through this maze

For us the unwritten rule was to listen and obey
To pay attention to what your parents had to say

They had their jobs to do; yours was to go to school
Back talk and disrespect weren't considered cool

I don't consciously remember being taught how it played
I just know that in school you learned and in church you prayed

No *sassing* your elders, those in authority *deserved* respect
When you didn't *behave* you knew what to expect

You knew what to do not to cook your own goose
It was a fear of sorts but not considered abuse

We knew instinctively not to cross "that" line
And look at us now, we all turned out fine

Wasn't it the greatest feeling when we were hugged?
The bottom line is we knew we were loved!

Hang In There!

I watched as the fog rolled in off the ocean
And there is a lesson here; I had a notion

Sometimes *we* are in a fog and can't see at all
Our burden is heavy; the sun we can't recall

It really *is* there; we just can't see it for a while
These tears *will* pass and be replaced by a smile

Sometimes, just as suddenly as a fog rolls in
It lifts and goes away, replacing our frown with a grin

We use up too much energy when we are sad and forlorn
We must learn to be patient and ride out the storm!

Patricia B. Schoeler

A Careless Word!

Oh, the power of a careless word
It hangs in the air; it has been heard

You can't take it back, no matter how hard you try
You would do anything to not make them cry

It's sort of like trying to *un-ring* a bell
Never been done, as far as I can tell

You can get your point across when done the proper way
So, please think carefully about what you say

It's worth the effort to *filter* your thought
To avoid all the sadness you inadvertently brought!

Dreams Fulfilled!

For every dream fulfilled, there is a broken heart
It's a lesson in life, an intricate part

It happens when teams or individuals compete
One leaves elated, the other in defeat

It happens at work when passed over for a promotion
We must mask our disappointment; not revealing our emotion

The thing we must learn is, not everyone can win
You did your best; carry this pride within

The fact that you made it this far says a lot
You accomplished it by giving everything you've got

Life is too short; it's not worth the strife
Enjoy what you do, have the time of your life!

Patricia B. Schoeler

It's OK!

We are only human, we may not always agree
On how things are or supposed to be

There doesn't always have to be a wrong or right
Perceptions aren't always the same, try as we might

To see both sides can actually be enlightening
And "different" doesn't need to be frightening

If agreement is not forthcoming, then try to compromise
Respect each other's opinions; not only smart but really wise!

One Victim; Many Casualties

When you read the paper, or watch the news on TV
Say a silent prayer for all those you cannot see

There are family and friends that are left behind
To grieve their loss, so much pain, you will find

Trying to figure out why, but it makes no sense
The enormity of it all is just so intense

There may be only one victim that we can see
But there are many casualties, you'd have to agree

Lives altered forever after a loved one falls
One victim, many casualties, is the truth of it all

Patricia B. Schoeler

Dance Like No One Is Watching!

Dance like no one is watching, let loose and have fun
You'll feel great when all is said and done

Get out there and enjoy yourself with total abandon
Dance with a partner or pick someone at random

Just feel the music and move with the beat
This is how some really great people get to meet

Join the crowd out there on the floor
They're just having a good time and nothing more

You may feel that "they're watching my every move"
The truth of the matter is they're just feeling the groove

Smile and laugh as if you haven't got a care in the world
You'll never know if you don't give it a whirl!

Private Thoughts

You know, it's really all about how we feel inside
Our own private thoughts, from the world we can hide

But these thoughts *do* control how we act
If you are happy, it shows, and that's a fact

It can be seen in the way we walk
It can be detected by our tone when we talk

Others can be affected by the mood we project
Think about the feedback we are sure to get

If we're happy, then they are too
If we are sad, they start to feel blue

When we're upset or angry, it can be seen on our face
Truth is, negative thoughts can be such a waste

We are missing the now, thinking about other things
Not enjoying the moment and the happiness it can bring!

Patricia B. Schoeler

Everything Has Changed!

For those who are hurting and left behind
Right now are in a terrible frame of mind

The world has changed and nothing feels right
And you think that there is no peace in sight

There are many reasons such as a death or divorce
Failed relationships, loss of a job - many reasons of course

Allow yourself to hurt and to feel the pain
But soon you need to pick yourself back up again

There are two choices that you can make
It's definitely not easy, so make no mistake

Either you feel sorry for yourself and feel pity every day
Or start to build a *different* life; it's the only way

You'll notice that others in your life continue to move along
It's a fact of life and it's not really wrong

Not that you are alone, but some things can only be accomplished by you
And just know that this *adventure* will take you along paths that are new

There is an inner strength that can carry you quite far
You'll be surprised at how strong you really are

However, your life may never be the same you will find
But new can be better if you keep an open mind!

Now The Journey Begins!

The wedding is over; this day is done
You're husband and wife, now united as one

Still individuals, but together you stand
To face your future, life can be grand

It can also be difficult; it can get rough
But ride the storms together; you are strong enough

Forgive each other and admit when you are wrong
Hug often, for in each other's arms you belong

Really mean it when you say, "this is my better half"
Know the wondrous feeling of sharing a good laugh

Today you really did marry your very best friend
To share everything with, until the very end!

Patricia B. Schoeler

Miracle Of Birth

Isn't it wonderful, this miracle of birth?
There is nothing to compare it to, on this earth

Their pending arrival leaves the parents glowing
For nine long months this baby is inside, sleeping and growing

When at last they meet, it's difficult to describe
The strong bonds of love are hard to hide

Life has changed profoundly; you will come to see
An awesome experience, the way it's supposed to be

It's a new responsibility that is scary but great
A challenge for sure, no one would debate

You'll get to rediscover things as you look through their eyes
The joy they get at every little surprise

This new little bundle that carries your name
From now on nothing will ever be the same!

Keep a smile on your lips
Warmth in your heart
And peace in your soul!

Patricia B. Schoeler

CHAPTER TWO

FAMILY WOES?

Here Goes!

Divorce

Divorce doesn't have to be ugly, don't make it that way
You loved each other once; remember your wedding day?

Through thick and thin, through sickness and health
Back then love was enough, that was your wealth

You would have done anything to protect each other from pain
To be happy and safe; you worked together for a mutual gain

Somewhere along the line your feelings must have changed
Sometimes *life* gets in the way and your goals get rearranged

Try talking it out to find out what went wrong
Isn't it worth the effort, you've been married so long?

Maybe too much has happened and now that love is lost
At least protect each other's pride at any cost

It's not necessary to be spiteful and mean and say terrible things
Words can't be taken back, think of the devastation they bring

Divide things fairly and move on if you must
No need to shred every last bit of trust

Remember your children and how this is causing them pain
Now acutely aware that nothing will be the same

They are learning the lesson that life's not always fair
Show them that you will always treat their feelings with care

Scared and alone, is what you are experiencing right now
Believe it or not you will make it through this somehow

Hold you head high and hang onto your dignity
You are stronger then you think, just wait and see!

Alcoholism

Alcoholism, in one way or another affects us all
Eventually it will set you up for a very hard fall

It really is a family disease
With outreaching effects you can't always see

Not only for the person that's caught in the grip
But the spouse that loves you, watching you slip

What about the kids who don't understand
Why you are no longer there to hold their hand

You may be there physically but emotionally you're not
How many promises are broken because you forgot?

Then there are your parents, it breaks their hearts
As they are forced to watch your life fall apart

What about your siblings who love you too
And only want to help and be there for you

Your close friends are also feeling the pain
Who long to see you safe and happy once again

Please stop and think about what you are doing
About the long term effects of this path you are pursuing

No one is judging you so have no fear
We just want you back to thinking clear

Hopefully soon you'll realize enough is enough
It's going to be hard, it's going to be tough

We will be there to help you in any way we can
To support and love you back to health once again!

Patricia B. Schoeler

Family Problems

It's a terrible thing when the family falls apart
It's like a stabbing pain in the heart

You never think it will happen to yours
Then seemingly out of the blue the unthinkable occurs

Feelings get hurt, angry words are spoken
Next thing you know someone's heart gets broken

So many incidents are brought up from the past
And accusations get flung so far and fast

Are things out of control, have they gone too far?
No one is happy with the way things are

The effects are felt by everyone in the family
Will things ever be the way they used to be?

Maybe the deep wounds will heal with time
And our family will once again be fine

We all have problems of this I'm well aware
And treating each other with respect is only fair

There is nothing so terrible that it can't be resolved
There is too much at stake, too much is involved!

Alzheimer's

Alzheimer's robs the person of who they once were
Thoughts and feelings once sharp are now a blur

Confusion sets in; they don't know who you are
Trapped in the past, sometimes back quite far

How frightening this must be for them; who do they know?
Everyone to them is a stranger, wherever they go

Some they see as nice, others are a threat
You wonder how much worse things will get

Their loved ones dealing with this are naturally stressed
Ever vigilant 24/7, too scared to take time to get some rest

The body is the same but the loved one has slipped away
It's like a slow death playing out before you, day by day

How painful for them to watch, for there is no cure
A devastating reality for everyone to endure!

Patricia B. Schoeler

Saying "I'm Sorry"

Why is it so hard to say, "I'm sorry" for something you have done
Is it because you believe you were the injured one?

Sometimes you need to sit back and take a real good peek
Do it honestly so you can gain the peace that you seek

There are two sides to every story and that's a fact
Be sure to listen to each other; it's too easy to get off the track

The longer things fester the harder it will be
To mend fences with your loved ones, you'd have to agree

You must decide now if it's worth all this pain
Try and discuss the problem so your relationship you can regain

It's not a sign of weakness you know, but one of strength
If deep down you care enough, you will go to any length

If it's a perceived wrongdoing from the past
How long is the *punishment* supposed to last?

We can't change it; it's been here and gone
We must deal with it *but* "for how long?"

Decide for yourself if it is worth the effort this will take
Peace and harmony are better than bitterness and heartbreak

Time that is lost can never be recovered
For many it was too late when this was discovered!

Left Behind

It's horrible to be the one that's left behind
You're no longer wanted; they've changed their mind

How could this happen, what went so wrong?
You want them with you where they belong

But they seem so happy to let go of the past
You're heart is broken; you thought it would last

All you want to do is sit down and cry
Trying to make sense of it, trying to figure out why

All their belongings are now removed from your home
Hurting so much as through the empty rooms you roam

There are no magic words that can console you right now
But you continue on finding the strength somehow

Things happen for a reason of which we may not be aware
But seek help and consolation from those who care

You *will* emerge from this stronger than before
And you'll learn to trust your heart once more!

Patricia B. Schoeler

Protect The Children!

It's so sad that kids become the casualties of "war"
When the adults in their life can't get along any more

What kind of example do we have them learning?
When hurtful accusations fly, as these bridges are burning

Kids learn by example, they look up to us
They know we love them so they give us their trust

If the relationship is irreversible and can no longer be fixed
Don't turn kids against loved ones; their feelings get mixed

If you withhold access to the kid's to get *your* own way
It's not realistic or fair; a heavy price to make them pay

Work on a solution; find a way they can be together
In a neutral setting for a while, it's not forever

It's worth the trouble; the rewards are high
For the sake of your children you should give it a try!

Hard to Watch!

It's hard to watch a child in pain
The reason for their distress is not always plain

Only they know what's going on in their mind
But they can't always tell us, you will find

Sometimes if we search, the reasons become clear
Other times even they may not know what's causing the fear

Others may suffer silently; they won't let it show
And this problem is more common than we may know

We love them so much and desperately want to do what's right
They need to know we're there for them, to help with this fight

It may take time, there is so much involved
But with love and patience, it can be solved!

Patricia B. Schoeler

Siblings

Forget the times when you didn't get along
In a certain period of time, when everything seemed wrong

Our raging hormones could make us laugh or cry
We were stretching our wings and trying to fly

It's a right of passage that we all go through
And I'll bet they have long ago forgiven you

Now you have grown up and headed out on your own
You may no longer live close but there is always the phone

Hold dear the family ties that bind
The results can be wonderful, you will find!

We only pass through this life once.
We are stronger than we think we are and can endure more than we may believe we can. Good things can come from bad situations if only we keep our minds open to new possibilities.

Patricia B. Schoeler

CHAPTER THREE

LOSS AND FAITH

Our Time of Grief

Times in the past when we would go to a wake
To the loved ones we would our condolences make

To the deceased we would pay our respect
To the family we would express our regret

We thought we knew exactly what to say
Spend some time and be on our way

We didn't think about when it's our time up there
In a state of shock and our soul's lying bare

People ask if there's anything we need,
And offer us advice we are expected to heed

There is no way we can comprehend what is being said
There is just so much running through our head

If you can help us with things behind the scenes
It would be appreciated; how much this would mean

It's the little details that can cause us a problem
You can think clearer, so please help us solve them

A hug, a smile and a reassuring hand
Say volumes of how much you understand

Please don't forget us after everything is over
I don't mean all the time; we don't need you to hover

Just remind us how much we still mean to you
That counts so much, if you only knew!

In The Blink of an Eye

From a wife to a widow in the blink of an eye
Reality hits and the impact makes you cry

At first there's a million things that you have to do
And everyone is around taking care of you

When everything settles down you are truly on your own
And it's now that you know the pain of being alone

The word *alone* has a whole new meaning
And if you're not careful it can send you reeling

But somehow you muddle through and come out stronger
You gain a new perspective and you're afraid no longer

Things that upended you before no longer do
You see things now from a different point of view

Remember and cherish the times you shared together
Your memories are yours to keep with you forever!

Patricia B. Schoeler

Nobody Knows For Sure!

We have no way of knowing what *actually* happens when we die
But our faith teaches us about Heaven and the commandments to live by

I think we all have our own perception of how it will be
And that happiness and beauty are all that we will see

We are told not to be afraid for we don't travel this journey alone
That love transcends death and that we are finally going home

We will never again feel pain; Heaven restores our health and youth
Enjoying our new "life" and finally learning the truth

For now, we must live and love every day we have here
It's God gift to us so hold every second dear

Do good, be good, laugh and love
God is smiling on us from up above!

So Unexpected!

(Suicide)

As with any unexpected death you go into shock
You know that it's true, but you pray that it's not

When someone you love commits suicide what can you say?
You wonder, what the reason was that made *them* act this way

You hurt from the pain of not saying goodbye
Your heart breaks because you may never know why

You ask, were there clues that I missed; was I totally inept?
Now these are circumstances you are forced to accept

Whatever drove them to commit this act?
There is no one to blame and that is a fact

We all react to *circumstances* in different ways
Some so horrendous we are left in a daze

Think about all of the past problems you have faced
Times so dark you were sure your happiness was erased

If you can't find a solution then you learn to cope
It's very important to *never* give up hope

It's a fact that the sun *always does* come out
Regardless of how you feel; it's what life is all about

Reach out to others important in your life
You need not be alone to face this strife!

Patricia B. Schoeler

So Young!

How can we explain the death of someone so young?
Especially when their life has just begun

The hurt you experience is deep and intense
For now nothing around you will make any sense

Perhaps there is another place this young soul needs to be
To spread love and laughter where we are unable to see

It's not for us to understand yet; it's best not to try
God is protecting this young soul so try not to cry!

A Tiny Soul

(Miscarriage)

A tiny little soul was getting ready to be born
But wasn't quite ready yet, so please don't mourn

Your hearts are heavy so great is your pain
Working through this together, stronger bonds you will gain

The reasons aren't always ours to know or understand
But I know the tiny soul is resting in God's loving hand!

Patricia B. Schoeler

Mom and Dad

Losing a parent can be hard to bear
Somehow we think they will always be there

We knew we were loved; they would be on our side
Our home was a safe place to run and hide

Even if we were wrong, we would be treated fair
To work through the problem, our burden they'd share

It's hard to lose the security of a parent's love
But trust they are safe in heaven above

It's OK to cry, it's a human emotion
To mourn their loss, to honor their devotion

Make them proud with all you have learned
That their trust in you was properly earned

It doesn't matter our age, whether young or old
We are still their *kids*, if truth be told!

Why?

When someone dies we try to make sense of it all
We're inconsolable as we feel our defenses fall

There is no way we can stop what is happening before our eyes
We try to be brave but our spirit cries

We speak of our pain and how it makes us feel
But something else is happening that our faith teaches us is real

It takes a long time to get to this spot
But through all of this, you do learn a lot

If we can relate this to the miracle of birth
Struggling to be *born,* for all we are worth

This time everyone is happy, and it's us that cry
But when we die it's reverse, ever wonder why?

God promises us a life everlasting, no pain or stress
Everlasting joy and love, a healing rest

We become young and strong, home where we belong
All ills are removed; we dance to a joyous song

Enjoy every day God gives us for it is a gift
There is always something there to give us a lift

A warm smile that's sent your way
The rainbow in the sky after a rainy day

A tender touch from someone you love
Whose love envelops you like a protective glove

Open your heart and open your mind
You'll be amazed at all the good you will find!

Patricia B. Schoeler

Thanks to our Veterans

For all the men and women serving our country, you make us proud
Because of you, we enjoy freedoms that other countries are not allowed

For all of the horrors you've faced, we can't begin to comprehend
Even when you return home, I'm sure these images don't end

How many times over fallen comrades have you prayed?
How can we possibly thank you for all the sacrifices you've made?

Fighting on foreign soil we pray for those who have fought and died
Because of you we can honor our flag with dignity and pride!

Pray For Our Soldiers!

Pray for our soldiers who have gone off to war
Protecting our freedoms is what they are fighting for

They give so much, these soldiers of ours
At a terrible cost, leaving many scars

They lose their youth, they've seen too much
Off on some battlefield and out of touch

Those who were wounded are changed forever
POW's face terrors of the worst kind ever

Those forced to kill others face another kind of pain
How can we expect our troops to be the same?

Losing their buddies causes them so much grief
How can we help them gain some relief?

Listen when they need to talk, give them some space
Welcome them back to a warm and safe place

Honor them with parades; show them we care
Thank them for fighting for us over there!

Patricia B. Schoeler

The Ultimate Sacrifice!

God bless those that have died on foreign soil
To their memories we will always remain loyal

Their lives were interrupted when they went off to war
They knew full well what they were fighting for

They were ready and willing when they got the call
And the sacrifices they made affect us all

Their heroism will benefit generations to come
Because they gave their lives so our freedom could be won!

A Change of Address

One bright, sunny day at the funeral for a friend
The priest advised "it's just the beginning, it's not the end"

Church Registries' write after their names "Rest in Peace"
Peace is what we'd wish for our loved ones at the very least

But to him he says, "It's just a change of address"
This is such a wonderful concept, I must confess

Everyone laughed when it was said by the priest
But it's a comforting thought for all of our deceased

Now they feel nothing but love as they laugh and they live
Wouldn't we want this for them if it were ours to give?

So we know they are happy in their new home
With their loved ones now and never alone

Life everlasting is what we are taught to believe
It's God's word so we must try not to grieve!

Patricia B. Schoeler

Beloved Pet

It's devastating to lose a beloved pet
For their love is the purest we will ever get

The perfect companion, both loving and fun
So excited to greet us when our day is done

Unconditional love, depending on us for every little thing
In return we love and protect them for the happiness they bring

They bring out the good in us, a soft and tender side
Listening to the hopes and dreams from others we may hide

Treasure every moment with them, every little wet kiss
Remember that every adoring look they give us really is bliss!

Learn from all that you have been through
Because it will make a stronger person of you
Take the time to reflect and pray
Remember to help others along the way
Be grateful for the times you've shared together
For memories of the heart can last forever!

God Bless

Patricia B. Schoeler

CHAPTER FOUR

LIFE'S LITTLE MOMENTS

Sandpipers

It's fun watching sandpipers on the beach
Within our sight but out of reach

Along the water's edge they go dancing and prancing
Unaware of us, standing there glancing

They haven't got a care in the world, is how it seems
We wish for the same peacefulness, in our dreams

Life is much more complicated, but that's OK
In the large scheme of things, it was designed this way

When things get too rough, visit this memory in your mind
It helps put things in perspective, you will find!

A Day At The Beach

The breeze over our bodies feels so good
The sun to soothe us just like it should

Who doesn't remember the smell of the salt sea air?
And lazy days on the beach, without a care

Watching kids laughing and playing happily in the sand
Or the smooth flight of the Sea Gulls as they come in to land

Combing the beach for sea shells with your friends
Enjoying the moment, wishing this would never end

The ocean has waves that are rough and fun
That toss and tumble you, dumping you when they are done

Sputtering salt water and with a bathing suit full of sand
A thrill that only a beach lover would understand!

Patricia B. Schoeler

Which Are You?

A morning person is like the light switch on the wall
Flip the switch and they're wide awake, no problem at all

Now, a night person, in the morning, is another story
Like a dimmer switch; turn slowly before reaching their glory

A morning person is bright and ready to talk
A night person barely has the energy to walk

Alertness comes eventually probably around 10
Becoming their bright selves once again

Come evening a night person is ready to go
But for the morning person, their weariness is starting to show

By 10pm they can barely stay awake, they are done for the night
The night person is perking along; everything is working out right

At least during the day, they are on common ground
Differences keep us on our toes, we have found!

A Dieter's Prayer

Lord, please help me make wise choices today
And skip temptations that come my way

I can't worry about yesterday, right or wrong
What I fed my face has been there and gone

But, I *can* control what I eat *this* day
Not worrying about tomorrow is the only way

Actually by taking it only one meal at a time
Should help me reach my goal, just fine!

Patricia B. Schoeler

Treadmill Time!

Get on the treadmill and do your time
Once in the habit it works out fine

Figure it's really your time alone
Watch TV or talk on the phone

Time to think or plan your dreams
It's really not as bad as it seems

Once you're done it really feels good
Those endorphins kick in as well they should

Makes you energized, makes you strong
Keeps you limber and moving along!

My Pup

A pet is an investment of the heart and mind
For a purer love you will never find

Unconditional love given every day
When not at your best, they love you anyway

There is an expression I would like to share with you
Think about these words, for they are ever so true

"May I become the kind of person my dog thinks I am"
Can you name one human who is a bigger fan?

They look at us through such adoring eyes
Of course we know they are very wise

Give them the gift of your love and your time
Play and cuddle them, the results are divine!

Patricia B. Schoeler

A Golfers Prayer

Rain, Rain go away
NEVER rain on a golfing day

Golfers get upset when they can't hit that ball
The weather must cooperate, it's an unwritten law

Business deals get made, problems get solved
It's not only a sport, there is so much involved

Walking is a great way to boost your health
Or ride in a covered cart if you have the wealth

Emotional well-being is guaranteed when things go well
But when shots go wrong? Hmmm, they'll never tell

Golfers are definitely a committed breed
So GO AWAY; give them the weather they need!

Hospitals At Night

Isn't this the truth?

It takes such a long time for us to fall asleep
And when we do, it seems so very deep

Then a hand on the shoulder shakes you awake
So sorry sweetie, but your temperature I must take

They tell you go back to sleep, you need your rest
It may take awhile but you try your best

A while later it's up again with the blood pressure cuff
Oh, please give us a break, enough is enough

If there's a logic to this, we fail to see
If we're asleep, can't you just let us be?

Patricia B. Schoeler

Puppies

Have you ever watched a puppy at play?
Leaping and frolicking and bouncing all day

Everything is wondrous, so much to see
Their biggest worry is scratching that flea!

Little vessels of unending love and trust
Only wanting to be with us, they could just about bust

They lick our faces and love us to death
Remember that smell of sweet puppy breath?

The round puppy belly that says it's full
And everything around is a toy he can pull

His sharp needle teeth leave tiny marks on your hand
This new home is an adventure; everything is just grand

He makes you laugh as he romps and plays
Guaranteed to chase all your troubles away!

Innocence of a Child!

The innocence of a child is such a pleasure to see
They react to things with laughter and glee

Life is an adventure, just so much fun
They have experienced so much when their day is done

Witnessing these little miracles is refreshing to the soul
We seem to lose this ability, as we grow old

Look, laugh, enjoy; let your "little kid" free
Always being serious is not how it's supposed to be!

Patricia B. Schoeler

Class Reunion

We attend class reunions to enjoy and relax
Re-new old friendships and that's a fact

We are aware that we have outwardly changed
Our bodies have now shifted and re-arranged

There is no need to hide from people we knew
They're just as concerned as me and you

Inside we are the same as we were before
Only more interesting now, we've lived so much more

We've all grown since those carefree days
Mature yes, but still kids in many ways

So enjoy reminiscing, laugh and dance
Don't regret it, by missing this chance!

Enjoy life's little moments,
the ones that make you smile or laugh.
These are the times that refresh us.
No matter how fleeting the moment,
they are there if you will take the time to see them.

Patricia B. Schoeler

CHAPTER FIVE

LESSONS LEARNED

A God Bless Day!

Every day we wake up is a God-bless day
We're given another chance to see what is heading our way

Hopefully it's something great and we'll do our best
Although sometimes our nerves are put to the test

Remember that God places us all where we need to be
The reasons aren't always apparent for us to see

Life is a mystery but it's fascinating all the same
So, relax and enjoy, that's the name of this game!

Kindness

Not many of us realize how many lives we lead
At home or out in the workplace trying to succeed

We play a different role in the lives of all we meet
Even when we offer a smile to a stranger on the street

Things we do can influence another person's day
By how we treat them and the tone of what we say

Be mindful of this, think before you act
Because an unkind word, can't really be taken back

But kindness goes such a long, long way
Makes everyone feel good, and have a good day!

Patricia B. Schoeler

Hi, It's Me!

Stand up to the world; say, "hi, it's me"
And what you'll get is what you see

Be proud of what and who you are
What you have to offer will carry you far

Success is measured on who we are inside
How we present ourselves to others, we alone must decide

Our own insecurities can sometimes get in the way
But there is so much out there, so seize the day

We're not all geniuses but we can be gentle, loving souls
To be decent, caring humans should be our ultimate goal

Take a chance on your dream; the most you can get is a NO
Because if you don't at least try, you may never know!

We May Never Know

We may never be aware of how many lives we touch
Or the number of people who love us so much

How many lives have we influenced along the way
Who will gather together for our funeral one day

Sharing stories of what we have done together
Tucked safely away in their memories forever

How wonderful to be remembered with a laugh and a smile
To know we meant something, that we were worthwhile!

Patricia B. Schoeler

Opportunity Knocks

When opportunity knocks, we know not where or when
Seize the moment, for it may never come again

Take a chance; just let it ride
Say hello to your playful side

It's good to be cautious; it's good to be smart
But sometimes you just need to follow your heart!

Self Centered!

Some people go through life thinking of themselves alone
Basing their worth on how many possessions they own

Never mindful of whom they may hurt along the way
As long as they come out first, at work or at play

What a lonely existence, they will some day find out
That you need family and friends; it's what life is about

If you are loved and respected and have your health
You can't ask for more; that's how to judge your wealth!

Patricia B. Schoeler

Jumping To Conclusions!

There is a great danger in jumping to conclusions
It can lead to misunderstandings and in general, confusion

Many times you can form a wrong impression
Because there may be details someone "forgot" to mention

There are invariably two sides to every story told
Preconceived ideas change as the tale unfolds

Obtain all the facts before you head off on your quest
Being well informed always works for the best!

The Ripple Effect

We are all responsible for our own actions
Some of which can set off a chain reaction

The danger of this; "The Ripple" effect
Affects others in ways you don't expect

It's like throwing a stone in the middle of a pond
The ripples start there, then spread way beyond

When something upsets you, your loved ones know
The stress and strain on you is sure to show

We may not be able to control this, but need to be aware
The consequences are felt by all who care!

Patricia B. Schoeler

Love Shouldn't Hurt!

You have given to another your heart and soul
A wonderful life together is your goal

A partner in life, someone you can always trust
A lover, confidant, best friend and fidelity is a must

When you look into their eyes, it makes you glad to be alive
You want to provide a safe haven where they may live and thrive

Protecting their feelings, no matter what the cost
The last thing you'd want is to have them hurt or feeling lost

When coming home, the joy you get, just knowing they are there
A secure and peaceful place, when life doesn't treat you fair

This emotion should be mutual for love to endure
When given without reservation, love is sweet and pure!

BUT IF;

Along the way things change and you no longer feel the same
Be honest enough to say so, this marriage is not a game

Discuss openly and freely any hurts or problems you feel
Because if they're not known to the other, how can you heal?

Never hurt or humiliate the other, allow them to save face
Remember what brought you together in the first place

Sometimes people grow apart and want different goals for their life
Or discover marriage isn't for them, no longer wanting to be husband and wife

If the marriage is to dissolve, always treat each other with respect
Both play fair and be adults, it's the least you should expect!

Family Ties!

The strength of family ties should never be underestimated
When you may feel that "tug" can never be anticipated

We grow up and think we can tackle the world all on our own
We are invincible; if need be we can handle anything alone

Life teaches us that friends may come and friends may go
But strong family ties sustain us, it's important to know

Sometimes it takes many bumps and bruises until we learn
When put to the test, families are there with their love and concern

A shared history can help in so many ways
As you laugh and remember "the good old days"

In the arms of your family, you are loved for who you are
Something to be contemplated before you stray too far!

Patricia B. Schoeler

Acceptance!

We learn through experience that acceptance is a state of mind
It's a hard road to travel, a difficult place to find

Try as we might there are just some things that cannot be changed
Our plans and dreams can get turned upside down and re-arranged

It's how we react to these changes, how we handle it now
We're in unfamiliar territory yet we survive it somehow

Change can be a good thing, taking us to places we may never have gone
New opportunities open up; we'll find a new comfort zone before long

Reach deep down inside yourself; you'll be surprised at what you find
Just give yourself a chance and be willing to keep an open mind!

We Never Know

We never know what life has to offer, what's coming our way
Or what hurtles or happiness we'll face during the day

We must trust in God that we are where we are supposed to be
Our path in life is not always clear to see

God in his wisdom knows what's best for us
Our faith teaches us to believe and to trust!

Patricia B. Schoeler

Roots and Wings

Oh the challenges parenthood brings
We want to give our kids roots but also wings

Roots give us stability; teach us where we belong
Loved for who we are, right or wrong

But you must also provide them with a set of wings
The sense of independence and freedom this brings

Supply them with the tools needed to go out on their own
To ease off on the "protection mode" to which we are prone

It's a delicate balance, not easy to reach
So many life lessons you want to teach

But we must trust in ourselves and hope for a job well done
Relax and enjoy the great adults they are sure to become!

Toxic People

Toxic people, we all know a few
Who seem to have a negative point of view

To them everything is wrong; nothing goes right
They see life as this terrible plight

Negative people can wear you down
They become so much work to be around

We can try and help them the best that we can
But when that doesn't work, well, it's time that we ran

We want to be around people who know how to have fun
Who are kind and positive, you feel good when this day is done

It feels much better for us to laugh than to cry
So, distance yourself from *The Toxic's,* you really must try!

Patricia B. Schoeler

Friends Can Let You Down

Sometimes friends can let you down
Turning your smile into a frown

Betrayal hurts, it's really rough
Sorting out emotions can be tough

Especially when it comes from out of the blue
Never expecting it, you're not sure what to do

It doesn't pay to be vengeful, to hurt just for spite
Just because they hurt you doesn't make it right

Words spoken in anger can never be taken back
And the person hearing them feels under attack

Now neither is listening to what's being said
They're just preparing a response in their head

If it can't be resolved you must let it go
The pain will eat you up; this you must know

Concentrate on the good things that give you pleasure
Don't waste another minute because each day is a treasure!

Life is such a wonderful gift. We should enjoy each and every day that
is given to us. Enjoy your family, your friends,
whatever it is that makes you happy.

It's so much easier to smile than it is to frown
Enjoy your life; don't let it get you down!

Patricia B. Schoeler

Personal prayer:

Thank you Lord for this gift you have given to me
The power and emotions of these words, you have allowed me to see
May I continue to help others in some small way
And give me the strength and courage I need each day!

www.ingramcontent.com/pod-product-compliance
Lightning Source LLC
Chambersburg PA
CBHW020919140626
46545CB00015B/892